William Mathias

Shakespeare Songs

Oxford University Press

Music Department, Great Clarendon Street, Oxford OX2 6DP

Commissioned by HTV Wales for the Cardiff Festival of
Choirs, this work was first performed on 8 February 1979 at the
Assembly Rooms, City Hall, Cardiff by The Dyfed Choir
conducted by John Davies with the composer as pianist.

Duration 16 minutes

Copies of this vocal score are also on hire.

To John Davies and The Dyfed Choir

SHAKESPEARE SONGS

WILLIAM MATHIAS
(Opus 80)

1. Under the Greenwood Tree

(AS YOU LIKE IT)

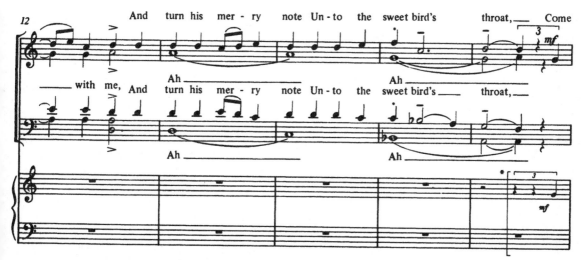

*The piano part in small notes here and elsewhere is optional, and only intended to assist vocal pitching. These sections should preferably be omitted in performance.

2. Who doth am - bi - tion shun, And loves to live ____ i' the sun,

Seek - ing the food he ___ eats, And pleas'd with what he gets, ____

Ah ____

Seek - ing the food he ___ eats, And pleas'd with what he ___ gets, ____ Come hi - ther, ____ come

Ah ____

Ah ____ Come hi - ther, ____

hi - ther, ____ come hi - ther, ____ come hi - ther, ____ come hi - ther, ____ come

come hi - ther, ____ come hi - ther, ____ come hi - ther, ____ come hi - ther,

hi-ther,_____ come hi-ther, come hi-ther, come hi-ther:_____ Here shall he see No

_____ come hi-ther, come hi-ther, come hi-ther:

e - nemy But win-ter, but win-ter, but__ win-ter and rough wea-ther, but win-ter and rough

wea-ther, but win-ter and rough _____ wea-ther. _____ (er!)

2. Full Fathom Five

(THE TEMPEST)

*Some Altos may be added to this line if so desired.

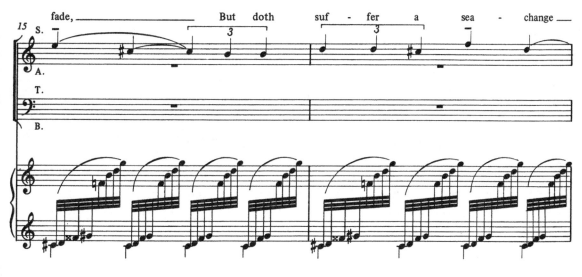

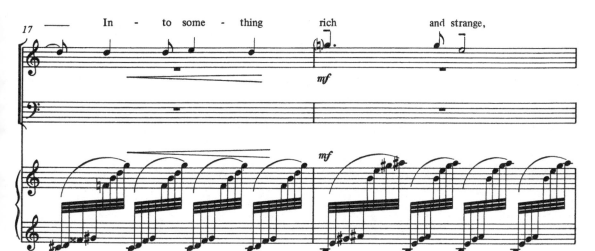

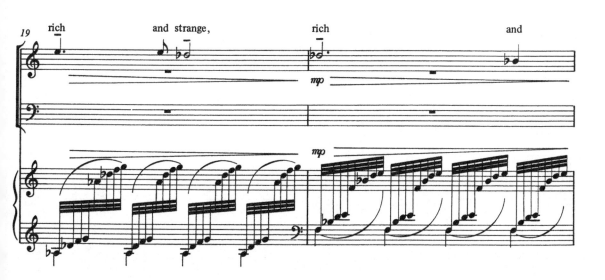

attacca

3. Lawn as White as Driven Snow

(THE WINTER'S TALE)

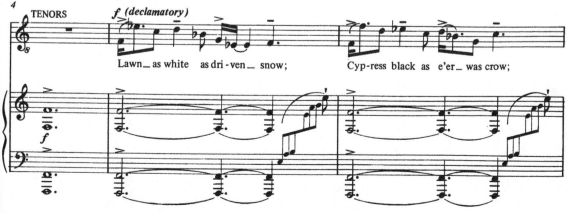

Lawn__ as white as dri-ven__ snow;   Cyp-ress black as e'er__ was crow;

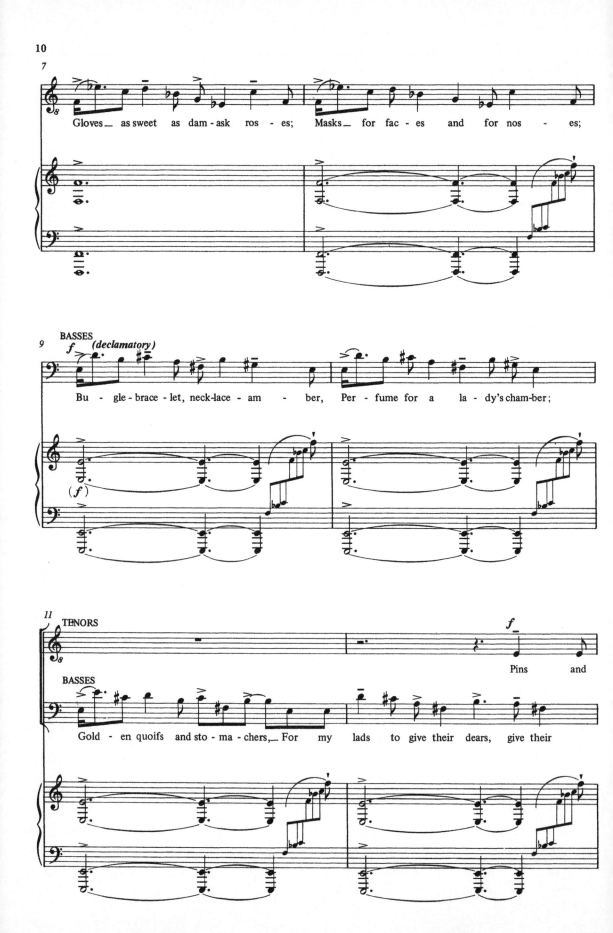

Gloves__ as sweet as dam-ask ros - es; Masks__ for fac-es and for nos — es;

BASSES
(declamatory)
Bu - gle-brace-let, neck-lace-am — ber, Per - fume for a la-dy's cham-ber;

TENORS
Pins and

BASSES
Gold - en quoifs and sto-ma-chers,__ For my lads to give their dears, give their

4. Sigh no more, Ladies

(MUCH ADO ABOUT NOTHING)

bon - ny,___ Con - vert - ing all your sounds of woe In - to Hey non-ny, non-ny, Hey non-ny, non-ny

bon - ny,___ Con - vert - ing all your sounds of woe In - to Hey non-ny, non-ny, Hey non-ny, non-ny,

Hey non-ny, non-ny, non - ny.___

Hey non-ny, non-ny, non - ny, non-ny.

Ah _____

2. Sing no more dit-ties, sing no moe___ Of dumps___ so dull and hea-vy;___ The

5. Crabbed Age and Youth

(THE PASSIONATE PILGRIM)

*(See note on page 1)

35

O! my love,— my love— is young:____ O! my love,— my love— is young:____

O! my love,— my love— is young:____ O! my love,— my love— is young:____

O! O! my love, my love is young:____ O! my love, my love is

O! O! my love, my love is young:____ O! my love, my love is

39

O! my love__ is young,— is young, is young, is young: Age, I do de-

O! my love __ is young,— is young, is young, is young: Age, I do de-

young,_____ is young,— is young, is young, is young: Age, I do de-

young,_____ is young,— is young, is young, is young: Age, I do de-

6. Dirge

(CYMBELINE)

Fear no more the frown o' the great, Thou art past the tyrant's stroke: Care no more to clothe and eat; To.

thee the reed is as the oak;— The scep-tre, learn-ing, phy-sic, must All fol-low this, and come to

dust._____ Fear no more the light-ning - flash,

7. It was a Lover and his Lass

(AS YOU LIKE IT)

† Only those adept at whistling. Alternatively, this part may be played by a group of recorders.

11 SOPRANOS

Sweet lov-ers love the spring.

ALTOS

T./B.

2. Be -

14

- tween the ac-res of the rye, With a hey, and a ho, and a hey no-ni- no, These pretty country folks would lie, In the

(sempre con ped.)   *(sim.)*

spring time, the on- ly pret - ty ring___ time, When birds do sing, hey ding a ding, ding;___

(whistling)

3. This

Sweet lovers love___the spring.___

Sweet lovers love the spring.

4. And

Sweet lov-ers love the spring.

there-fore take the pres-ent time, With a hey, and a ho, and a hey no - ni - no; For

4. And there-fore take the pres-ent time, With a hey, and a ho, and a hey no - ni -

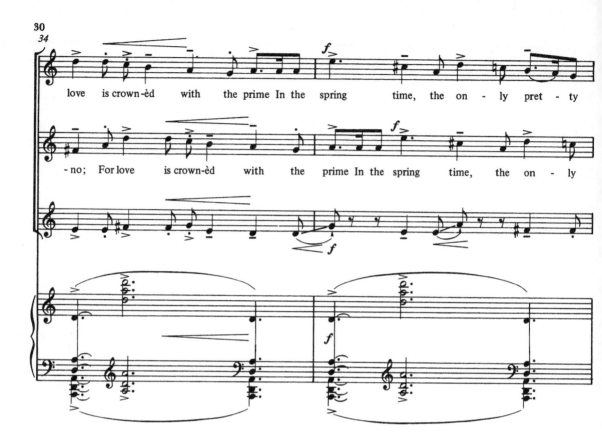

sweet lov-ers love___ the spring.___

sweet lov-ers love___ the spring.

attacca

8. Blow, blow, thou Winter Wind

(AS YOU LIKE IT)

1. Blow, blow, thou

win-ter wind,_____ Thou art not so un-kind_____ As man's in-grat-i-tude;

Thy tooth is not so keen,_____ Be-

Thy tooth is not so

Thy tooth is not so keen,_____ Be-

Thy tooth is not so

-cause thou art not seen,_____ Al-though thy breath be rude._____

keen,_____ Be-cause thou art not seen,_____ Al-though thy breath be

-cause thou art not seen,_____ Al-though thy breath be rude.

keen,_____ Be-cause thou art not seen,_____ Al-though thy breath be

This life___ is most jol - ly.

2. Freeze, freeze, thou bit - ter sky,___ That dost not bite so nigh___ As

Though

ben - e - fits for-got:

Though

thou the wa-ters warp, _____ Thy sting is not so sharp _____ As

Though thou the wa-ters warp, _____ Thy sting is not so

thou the wa-ters warp, _____ Thy sting is not so sharp _____ As

Though thou the wa-ters warp, _____ Thy sting is not so

friend re - mem - bered not. _____

sharp _____ As friend re - mem-bered not. _____

friend re - mem.- bered not. _____

sharp _____ As friend re - mem-bered not.

38

Reproduced and printed by
Halstan & Co. Ltd., Amersham, Bucks., England